COPING™

COPING WITH

EATING DISORDERS

Carmen Cusido

Rosen
YA™

New York

Published in 2019 by The Rosen Publishing Group, Inc.
29 East 21st Street, New York, NY 10010

First Edition

Library of Congress Cataloging-in-Publication Data

Names: Cusido, Carmen, author.
Title: Coping with eating disorders / Carmen Cusido.
Description: First edition. | New York : Rosen YA, 2019. | Series: Coping | Audience: Grades 7–12. | Includes bibliographical references and index.
Identifiers: LCCN 2018016579| ISBN 9781499467154 (library bound) | ISBN 9781508183174 (pbk.)
Subjects: LCSH: Eating disorders—Treatment—Juvenile literature.
Classification: LCC RC552.E18 C875 2019 | DDC 616.85/2600835—dc23
LC record available at https://lccn.loc.gov/2018016579

Manufactured in China

CONTENTS

INTRODUCTION

Growing up, *Full House* star Candace Cameron Bure had a healthy body image, but that changed when the then twenty-year-old actress moved from California to a Canadian city where she didn't know many people. The problems arose for Bure soon after she stepped away from the Hollywood spotlight after marrying her ice hockey–player husband, Valeri Bure, in 1996. The actress said she "turned to food for comfort," and that unhealthy relationship turned into a bout with bulimia.

"I dealt with [bulimia] for several years but it wasn't about body image and trying to feel good—it was about trying to find comfort or fill voids within myself," the actress told *ET* in a 2016 interview. "I was sitting in church and I was by myself, my husband was on the road. The sermon somehow just spoke to my heart and that's when I went directly to my pastor and said, 'I need help' … That was the moment that I went, 'I don't want to do this anymore.'"

Bure, who now stars in *Fuller House* on Netflix, is a spokesperson for the Eating Recovery Center and was an ambassador for the center's first Eating Recovery Day when it launched in 2016. By speaking out about her experience with bulimia, Bure hopes to illustrate

Actress Candace Cameron Bure has been outspoken about her past struggle with bulimia. She has become a recovery ambassador for the Eating Recovery Center.

that it is possible to recover from an eating disorder. It may take time and treatment though.

Eating disorders include well-known illnesses such as anorexia nervosa, bulimia nervosa, and binge eating disorder, as well as some much rarer conditions. About thirty million people in the United States will experience eating disorders in their lifetimes, and these disorders are the third-most common chronic illnesses in adolescents, according to the American Academy of Pediatrics. In Canada, nearly one million people meet the diagnostic criteria for an eating disorder, according to the National Eating Disorder Information Centre. Eating disorders are the most common chronic illnesses among female adolescents, with up to 5 percent of that population affected, according to Hopewell, a nonprofit eating disorder support center based in eastern Ontario.

Eating disorders can be triggered by a number of factors. Some people are genetically predisposed to starve themselves or binge and purge or become susceptible to other disordered eating behaviors. Some people suffer from eating disorders because they have low self-esteem and body-image issues— for example, a person might see herself as fat when she is actually a normal weight or underweight. Other times, eating disorders are triggered by traumatic events such as physical or sexual abuse or the loss of a loved one.

Although eating disorders are a huge problem for many people, it is possible to overcome these illnesses. There are various effective treatments that can pave the way for recovery. Whether you think you may have an eating disorder yourself or are concerned about a loved one with disordered eating habits, it is important to learn the facts about eating disorders in order to understand how to cope with them.

CHAPTER ONE

Understanding Eating Disorders

The most common eating disorders diagnosed in the United States are anorexia nervosa, bulimia nervosa, and binge eating disorder (BED), though there are a number of other conditions that are recognized by the *Diagnostic and Statistical Manual of Mental Disorders*, 5th edition (DSM-5). Published by the American Psychiatric Association since the 1950s, this manual defines mental illnesses in order to improve their diagnoses, treatment, and research.

Eating disorders are serious mental illnesses that can severely impact a person's physical and emotional health and can impair the person's ability to function in everyday life. The conditions often develop in adolescence and young adulthood, though people of all ages have been diagnosed with eating disorders.

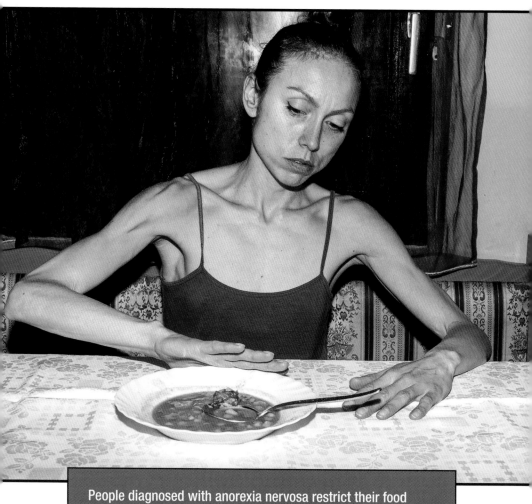

People diagnosed with anorexia nervosa restrict their food intake or eat only certain foods and avoid others. While it is often associated with young girls, anorexia can affect anyone.

Symptoms vary based on the type of eating disorder, but generally these illnesses can cause serious damage to the heart, bones, digestive system, teeth, and mouth and can lead to other complications, diseases, and even death.

What Is Anorexia Nervosa?

One of the three main types of eating disorders, anorexia nervosa is manifested when individuals refuse to maintain the minimal weight for their body mass index, restrict their food intake, have a distorted body image and an intense fear of becoming fat (typically weighing themselves repeatedly), and have an abnormal fear of food.

A person with anorexia may not exhibit all the signs and symptoms of the disease right away. Some of the emotional and behavioral signs of the illness include drastic weight loss; dressing in layers to hide the weight loss or to stay warm; a preoccupation with dieting, fat grams, weight, and calories; refusing to eat certain foods; denying feeling hungry; developing food rituals, such as eating foods in certain orders or rearranging food on a plate; cooking meals for others but not eating; frequently making excuses to avoid situations involving food; social withdrawal; and loss of menstrual periods in adolescents and adults.

Physical symptoms that develop over time include stomach cramps, difficulty concentrating, muscle atrophy (when muscles waste away), dizziness and fainting, sleep problems, feeling cold often, anemia, brittle hair and nails, dry and yellowish skin, low blood pressure, and brain and heart damage.

Though anorexia typically begins in adolescence, the disorder can affect people of any age, gender, sexual orientation, economic background, and ethnicity.

Good Morning America meteorologist Ginger Zee began a four-year battle with anorexia after her parents divorced when she was ten years old. In her book, *Natural Disaster: I Cover Them. I Am One*, Zee wrote

ABC News chief meteorologist Ginger Zee has opened up about her past struggle with anorexia, an eating disorder she struggled with from ages ten to fourteen.

that she "didn't choose to get anorexia, but the choice you do have is asking for help." Zee, who has now recovered from her eating disorder, credits her mother and stepfather with helping her overcome anorexia. "It didn't make me better right away, but I knew I had the great support of my family," Zee told *People* magazine in 2016.

Connie Inglis developed a severe case of anorexia at age ten and had to be hospitalized three times in nine years. Now in her twenties, she uses social media to document her recovery. She posts photos of herself on Instagram to promote body confidence and encourage people with eating disorders to keep working on recovery.

Inglis wrote on Instagram to people who are currently suffering from anorexia:

> *I had given up. My eating disorder had taken over and I wanted to die. But the people I loved stayed by me ... For the first time in my life I realised that I loved these people more than my ed [eating disorder]. So I fought, I fought like hell ... Yes I still have the thoughts. But I am strong enough now to resist! Keep going! We can do this together!*

What Is Bulimia Nervosa?

Bulimia nervosa is an illness that is characterized by binge eating—consuming a large quantity of food in a short time—followed by purging. Purging most commonly means vomiting, but it can also include using laxatives, diuretics, and enemas. Some people with bulimia don't purge, but they use other calorie-ridding methods such as fasting, dieting, or exercising excessively.

Signs and symptoms of the disorder include a preoccupation with body shape and weight; fear of gaining weight; using laxatives, diuretics, and enemas after eating to get rid of food and for rapid weight loss; feeling a loss of control over one's eating behavior; eating until feeling uncomfortably full; and eating more during a binge episode than a normal-sized meal or snack.

Unlike people who are diagnosed with anorexia, bulimics often have a normal body weight. And unlike people with BED, bulimics vomit or find other ways to get rid of food after eating.

While recovery from bulimia—as with any eating disorder—is possible, some people may struggle with the illness for years after its initial onset. Singer and actress Demi Lovato underwent rehab not just for her struggle with bulimia but also for her drug and alcohol addictions in 2010. In her YouTube documentary, *Simply Complicated,* Lovato revealed that things were out of control during her teen years while she was working at the Disney Channel and touring with the Jonas Brothers. While she has conquered

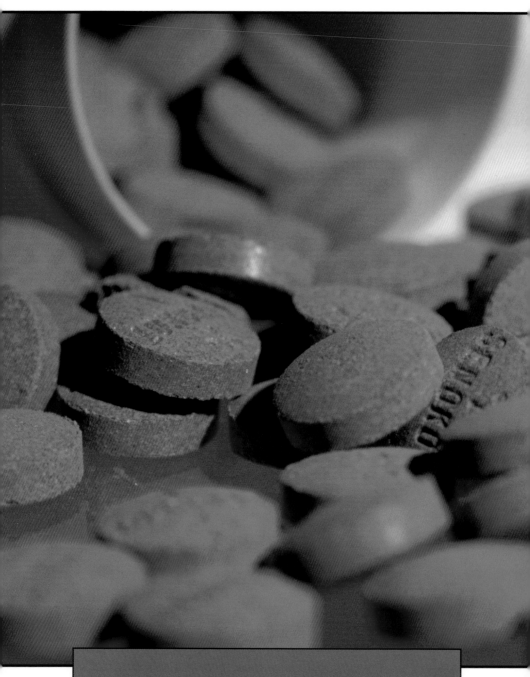

People with bulimia nervosa often binge eat and then purge, either by making themselves throw up or by abusing laxatives.

her addictions, Lovato said she continues to struggle with an eating disorder.

"I haven't relapsed in drugs and alcohol," Lovato recalled in *Simply Complicated*. "That's something that I'm very proud of … but one thing I haven't fully conquered is my eating disorder. The less I have to think about food, the easier it is for me to go about having a normal life."

According to a small study reported in the *Journal of Abnormal Psychology*, the brains of women with bulimia use food to avoid negative thoughts about themselves. Researchers fed twenty women— ten with bulimia and ten without— the same meal before showing them a series of neutral images followed by photographs of high- fat or high-sugar foods like pizza or brownies while scanning their brains. All participants were given impossible math problems to solve to make them stressed. They were then shown the pictures of food and asked to rate their stress and food-craving levels.

Though everyone's stress levels had gone up while attempting to solve the math problems, the scans of bulimic women showed very different results. Blood flow to the precuneus region of the brain decreased for women with bulimia when they looked at pictures of food. A second study with seventeen bulimic participants showed the same results.

"We found that it doesn't take much stress to trigger binge-eating," Sarah Fischer, a professor at George Mason University and the coauthor of the study, told the BBC. "I would love to see if teaching basic emotion-regulation behavioral skills works for some women. For others, they may need medication or transcranial stimulation to stop the rise in stress before they binge."

Untreated bulimia can severely impact a person's health and can be potentially life threatening. According to the Mayo Clinic,

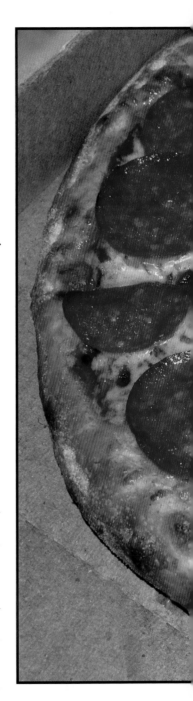

Stress can trigger binge eating in people with bulimia, who often use food as a way to avoid negative feelings about themselves.

complications from bulimia include dehydration—which can lead to major medical problems like kidney failure, heart problems, severe tooth decay, and gum disease—irregular menstrual periods, anxiety and depression, digestive problems, and misuse of drugs or alcohol.

What Is Binge Eating Disorder?

Unlike bulimia nervosa, individuals diagnosed with BED eat large quantities of food in a short period of time, but they do not purge or find other ways to get rid of that food. People with BED also eat when they're not hungry, frequently eat alone or in secret, and feel depressed, guilty, or upset about eating.

The disorder was officially recognized as an illness in 2013 by the *DSM-5*. It had previously been listed under the category eating disorder not otherwise specified (EDNOS). Now that BED is officially codified, people can be screened and treated for this disorder, which is underdiagnosed and undertreated, according to the Binge Eating Disorder Association.

Anyone can overeat on occasion, but for those with BED, excessive overeating becomes a regular occurrence and feels out of control. The Mayo Clinic has listed several risk factors that can increase the likelihood of developing BED. They include family history (you're more likely to have an eating disorder if your siblings or parents have had them), mental health issues, dieting, and age. BED typically begins in the late teens or early twenties, though both young children and older adults have been diagnosed with the disorder, according to the National Eating Disorders Association (NEDA). Many people with BED are overweight or obese, but others may be normal weight.

Some of the complications that may develop with BED include obesity and medical conditions related to obesity such as sleep-related breathing disorders, joint problems, heart disease, type 2 diabetes, and gastrointestinal issues. Sometimes psychiatric disorders are linked to BED. They include depression, anxiety, bipolar disorder, and substance abuse disorders.

Actress Lynn Chen, a New Jersey native raised by Taiwanese parents, told NPR in 2015 that she received mixed messages about food as a child: she was encouraged to eat large amounts of food but remain thin. Over the years, she struggled with binge eating. She had what she called "last supper" days, when she'd begin overeating in the morning and continue through to the evening.

"It could have been carrots and hummus or cookies, whatever was easy to eat. Some days, I was on a set where there were snacks as far as the eyes can see. I'd be eating my feelings all day long," Chen recounted. She would sometimes involuntarily throw up for days after

Actress Lynn Chen developed binge eating disorder after receiving confusing messages about food as a child. She would go through periods of binge eating and periods of starvation.

consuming large quantities of food without pausing. The excessive eating led to periods of starvation, and Chen said she briefly struggled with anorexia as well.

Chen said she's curbed her BED and has a healthier relationship with food. On a recent trip to Taiwan, Chen became assertive when she felt the tour guide was shaming her for not eating all the food she was served. "I told her, 'listen, I have an eating disorder. I'm not eating more than I feel comfortable with.'"

Effects of Social Media on Eating Disorders

Social media platforms ranging from Facebook to Snapchat can serve as vehicles to connect with classmates and loved ones, but they can also serve as a catalyst for eating disorders, particularly for individuals who are bullied into starving themselves or bingeing and purging by their peers. Seeing images of waif-thin models or friends or finding

(continued on the next page)

(continued from the previous page)

hashtags that promote "bonespiration" (celebration of extremely thin bodies) can fuel a person's desire to count calories, exercise incessantly, or eat large quantities of food and then throw up. The NEDA has found that up to 65 percent of people with eating disorders say bullying "contributed to their condition."

If you find that social media is triggering unhealthy eating habits, try using social media as a means to empower yourself instead of fueling your low self-esteem. A way to achieve that is to unfollow bullies

Instead of looking at images that make you feel bad about yourself, seek out body positive messages on social media by using hashtags like #foodisfuel.

who may trigger disordered eating behavior. Rather than celebrating unhealthy bodies, try looking for positive images using hashtags like #edrecovery and #foodisfuel. Another approach is to unplug from social media completely for a while.

Other Eating Disorders

The most common eating disorders are anorexia, bulimia, and BED, but there are a few lesser-known but equally serious eating disorders listed in the *DSM-5*. These include avoidant/restrictive food intake disorder (ARFID), pica, and rumination syndrome. The addition of these eating disorders to the *DSM-5* has led to more awareness of these rare conditions and increased opportunities to treat them.

Avoidant/Restrictive Food Intake Disorder

ARFID was added to the *DSM-5* in 2013 and is similar to anorexia in that both illnesses involve limiting the amount—and types—of food eaten. However, unlike anorexia, people with ARFID do not fear being fat or have preoccupations with body shape and size.

While many children undergo phases of selective or picky eating, someone with ARFID has these issues every day, at every meal, and it can interfere with his or her daily life. A person diagnosed with this eating disorder does not eat enough to grow and develop properly, and in adults it becomes difficult to maintain basic body function, according to the NEDA.

Some of the characteristics of the illness include significant weight loss (or failure to achieve expected weight gain in children), significant nutritional deficiency, a dependence on nutritional supplements, and a marked interference with psychosocial functioning. Researchers have found that many children with the disorder avoid food and have decreased appetite, abdominal pain, and sometimes a fear of vomiting. Since not much research has been done into ARFID, it is unclear how common the illness is.

Other warning signs that a person may have ARFID include dramatic weight loss, dressing in layers to hide weight loss or to stay warm (people with too little body fat often have a hard time maintaining their body temperature), vague but consistent complaints of an upset stomach or of feeling full around mealtimes, the loss of menstrual periods, only eating foods with certain textures, lack of interest in food, and a limited range of preferred foods that become narrower over time. However, people with ARFID do not have any body-image issues or fear of weight gain.

"A large issue I see is avoiding foods based on certain textures, smell or even brands of food," Kristina Zufall, a psychologist who specializes in eating disorders, said in an interview with Romper in 2018. "Limited food intake and weight loss can cause malnutrition which may be evident in lab work conducted at physicals. When physical causes are ruled out, ARFID may be a cause."

Treatment for ARFID may include behavioral and psychological interventions such as exposure therapy and cognitive behavioral therapy.

Pica

Pica is characterized by the desire to eat inedible items such as soap, dirt, clothes, or other items that don't provide any nutritional value. The diagnosis often occurs with other mental health disorders such as schizophrenia, an intellectual disability, or an autism spectrum disorder.

Thirteen-year-old Jade Noakes, from New York, has been hospitalized several times after eating items like sand, paper towels, and erasers. Jade, who also has autism, has had bouts of alcohol poisoning from drinking hand sanitizer and lead poisoning "from eating several pencils in a two-day time span," according to her mother, Nicole Noakes, who was interviewed by the Daily Mail. "She has no idea she is doing it. For Jade it is like needing a glass of water when you are extremely thirsty," Nicole Noakes added. Her goal is to raise money for a therapy dog for her teenage daughter to help her keep from eating things she shouldn't.

In India, surgeons removed a total of 15 pounds (6.8 kilograms) of metal foreign objects from a thirty-five-year-old man's stomach. Doctors found 3 pounds (1.4 kg) of nails, a 6-inch (15.2-centimeter) piece of rusted iron shackle, hundreds of coins, dozens of shaving blades, and shards of glass and stones. "Frequently, these actions [of eating foreign objects] help to calm the individual," according to psychiatrist Ken Yeager, director of the Ohio State University Wexner Medical Center's Stress, Trauma and Resilience Program. "There is a connection with anxiety, and many who have anxiety also suffer from depression at times," he added.

Author Sera L. Young offered a hypothesis for pica in her book,

Pica is an eating disorder that is characterized by eating nonfood items that provide no nutritional value, such as hair, dirt, nails, and other substances.

Craving Earth: Understanding Pica. She suggested eating inedible items may be a way for some people to get nutrients they're typically missing from their diets. For example, someone who is iron deficient may crave dirt. Treatment involves first addressing any nutrient deficiencies or other medical issues, such as lead poisoning, followed by behavioral therapy, mild aversion therapy, or in some cases, medication to treat an associated developmental disorder.

Rumination Syndrome

Rumination syndrome is a rare eating disorder characterized by regularly regurgitating food. A person who repeatedly regurgitates food for a period lasting at least a month fits the criteria to be diagnosed with this condition. The illness is a subconscious reflex, not a conscious decision, and researchers do not know what causes this syndrome.

Rumination is different from vomiting in that the food is undigested and often still tastes the same as when it was first eaten, according to the Children's Hospital of Philadelphia. Though the regurgitation is subconscious, researchers have found that the voluntary muscle relaxation of the diaphragm becomes a learned habit.

Sometimes, doctors diagnose rumination syndrome simply by looking at a patient's medical history, asking about symptoms, and observing the person's behavior. Other times, physicians may perform tests to rule out other causes of regurgitation. In one test, called an esophagogastroduodenoscopy, a doctor inspects the esophagus and the upper part of the small intestine to search for any obstruction that could cause regurgitation. Another procedure, called gastric emptying, determines how long it takes a marker food to leave the stomach.

Treatment for rumination syndrome involves relearning how to digest food, which can be taught by a behavioral therapist.

Myths & FACTS

Myth: Eating disorders are a choice, and people should just snap out of it.

Fact: Nobody chooses to have an eating disorder. Decades of genetic research have shown that biological factors play a big role in determining who may develop an eating disorder. Eating disorders are complex psychiatric and medical illnesses. They often coexist with other conditions like anxiety, depression, social phobias, and obsessive-compulsive disorders.

Myth: Anorexia is the only life-threatening eating disorder.

Fact: Eating disorders are the deadliest forms of mental illness, according to the National Association of Anorexia Nervosa and Associated Disorders. All eating disorders can be life threatening and can do long-term physical and psychological damage.

Myth: Men and boys don't get eating disorders.

Fact: Men and boys make up about one-third of the people diagnosed with eating disorders in the United States. That means ten million men and boys will suffer from an eating disorder at some point in their lives, according to the NEDA. In fact, men with eating disorders may face additional stigma for having a disorder that is characterized as feminine, and they may be less likely to seek help for it.

CHAPTER TWO

What Triggers Eating Disorders?

One common misconception about eating disorders is that people who suffer from them are seeking attention or lack willpower. The reality is that there are several factors—biological, psychological, interpersonal, and social—that may contribute to the onset of these mental illnesses. Some eating disorders manifest themselves when people's obsession with food and weight leads them to take actions that ultimately disrupt their health, relationships, and daily activities.

Sometimes, a specific situation can trigger eating disorders for people who are vulnerable. For example, some athletes may have to maintain a low body weight to compete. Similarly, teens may succumb to peer pressure to lose a few pounds but then use unhealthy methods, such as starving themselves or vomiting after eating, to

Sometimes a specific situation can trigger eating disorders for those who are vulnerable. Dancers may be pressured into losing weight to perform, which can lead to disordered eating.

achieve that goal. Traumas such as abuse, rape, or the death of a loved one may trigger an eating disorder. Other triggers include body-image issues and Western cultural ideals and pressures to be thin, particularly for girls and women. Failure to understand the underlying causes of eating disorders can lead to stigma, which makes it more challenging to seek effective treatment.

Genetics

Genetic factors can contribute to the onset of eating disorders, according to a 2017 study by researchers at Michigan State University. People whose family members have had an eating disorder are more likely to develop eating disorders themselves.

Some heritable traits—obsessive thinking, a tendency to be a perfectionist, impulsiveness, hypersensitivity, and emotional instability—tend to precede the onset of an eating disorder. Scientists from the University of Iowa and the University of Texas Southwestern Medical Center studied individual families that had a history of eating disorders across generations. They concluded that mutations in two specific genes cause, respectively, 90 percent and 85 percent of people with those mutations to develop an eating disorder. Michael Lutter, a psychiatrist for the Eating Recovery Center, assistant professor of psychiatry at the University of Iowa, and the senior author of the study, reports that "the most useful thing is that [this research] will allow us to study the neurobiology, the underlying cause of eating disorders, and try to find new ways to boost the pathway to prevent them."

In a 2017 study published in *PLOS One*, a scientific journal, Lutter sequenced the genes of ninety-three unrelated people with eating disorders: some binge ate, and others restricted their food. He discovered two specific links in two different genetic variations. The variant found in the people who restricted their food is called neurotensin. It regulates appetite and tells the body it needs more food. The variant found in those who engaged in binge eating is glucagon-like peptide 1, a hormone released by the gastrointestinal system that tells people when they're full after eating.

"Right now there's no way to use genetics to guide treatment but it does offer a better understanding of the pathophysiology of the illness that we can do these studies and measure levels of these hormones," Lutter told the Daily Beast in 2018. He believes it may be possible to develop genetics-based treatment for eating disorders in the future.

Heading to College

The freedom of being on one's own for the first time can be exciting, but for someone with an eating disorder or someone who is recovering from one, going away to college could present challenges regarding how much— or how little—to eat and how much to exercise. The stress that arises from trying to do well in school can also make someone with an eating disorder vulnerable to acting out with unhealthy behaviors. And when meals conflict with class times, it can lead some to skip out on eating.

It's important to remember that disordered eating is not the same thing as having an eating disorder.

Heading to college may trigger an eating disorder relapse. It can be hard to establish a healthy eating routine in a new environment.

While many college students may eat at strange times or in strange ways, this doesn't mean they have an eating disorder. "An eating disorder actively interferes with your ability to have a life," according to dietitian Valerie Bryden at Walden Behavioral Care. One example would be turning down a meal invitation with a friend because you're starving yourself.

While the pressure to reach an ideal weight and size remains, some college students are literally smashing that unhealthy model and replacing it with messages of body positivity. At an event called the Southern Smash at the University of Virginia in 2016, students destroyed scales with baseball bats. They also had a chance to write their "perfect" number on a balloon—be it weight, grades, or calories—and release it, symbolizing letting go of those ideals. "It is important for young women to understand their worth is not in their weight," said third-year college student Kendall Siewert.

Coping with Eating Disorder Triggers

Here are some tools that can help you deal with eating disorder triggers.

Ask friends to keep you accountable. Tell a friend what unhealthy behaviors to look for and how to approach you if she notices any of them.

Sometimes it's healthier to donate clothes that no longer fit you than to trigger eating disorder behaviors by keeping them and trying to lose weight so you can wear them again.

Get rid of old clothes. It's better to let go of items that don't fit anymore than to attempt to lose weight in order to fit into them.

Stop comparing yourself to others. Practice self-love and compassion instead.

Seek support from your community. If you belong to a sorority, fraternity, faith community, or any other group, consider asking other members for help, or eat meals and go grocery shopping as a group.

Identify resources. If you need additional help, consider attending support groups and seeking mental health counseling at your college campus.

Personality

Authors Stephanie Cassin and Kristin von Ranson reviewed a decade of research into the personalities of people with anorexia, bulimia, and BED. In their widely referenced 2005 study, they argue that personality plays a pivotal role in each of these illnesses and that the same set of traits is frequently associated with certain eating disorders. For instance, anorexics tend to have high levels of harm avoidance, which is characterized by worrying, pessimism, and low levels of novelty seeking, while bulimics are typically impulsive and have high levels of novelty seeking. Some obsessive-compulsive personality traits that are found in people with anorexia and people with bulimia include inflexibility, perfectionism, a drive for order and symmetry, and excessive doubt and cautiousness. Those diagnosed with BED have less well-defined personality traits.

However, just because people exhibit certain personality traits does not mean they're destined to suffer from an eating disorder. Other factors, such as being bullied by peers, feeling stressed at school, and feeling pressure to diet and embody the media's portrayal of the ideal body as thin, are also vital in determining whether a person will develop an eating disorder.

Self-Esteem and Body-Image Issues

Body image is how a person feels about his or her own body—including weight, height, and shape. People with positive body image appreciate and celebrate their bodies and feel that their shape does not determine their character or value as people. People with poor self-esteem and negative body image may have a distorted view of their shape and size: how they

Some people with body-image issues may compare themselves to models and celebrities they see in magazines and on television, social media, and elsewhere.

perceive themselves does not match reality. Some may idolize people who are thin and strive to lose weight in an unhealthy way.

John Kirby, CNN's military analyst, and his daughter Meagan McDowell, who suffered from anorexia for many years, wrote an op-ed for CNN about how the media's focus on thinness continues to set unrealistic

41

expectations for young women. The father-daughter duo wrote:

> It's a toxic environment, made all the more so by the instant, constant and persistent access to unhealthy ideas and imagery propagated online and through social media. It's too easy to shame or bully a young girl on Twitter or Snapchat. It's too easy for them to feel inadequate as a result of swimsuit advertising, diet programs and entertainment vehicles propagating "ideal" shapes and sizes for women.

But Kirby and McDowell also point out that some of that toxicity is starting to change: there are increasing numbers of plus-size women hired as models, and women of all shapes and sizes are beginning to get more visibility in leading roles in Hollywood.

Egyptian Canadian blogger Mina Gerges shared his struggles with body-image issues and his three-year battle with eating disorders with his 145,000 Instagram followers during Eating Disorder Awareness Week in February 2018. Gerges said unrealistic standards for the male body led to his struggle. He wrote:

> I grew up surrounded by unrealistic pictures of men and women that convinced me that I have to look like that to be considered attractive and desirable. Especially as gay men, where unfortunately so many of us struggle

with achieving that unrealistic standard to feel beautiful. Trying to achieve this made me develop an eating disorder when I was 20—I would starve myself, weigh myself every morning, spend 3 hours at the gym and ran 10km every day, and hated myself if I ate something "unhealthy," and still, never found happiness or satisfaction.

How to Spot a Potential Eating Disorder in a Loved One

If you are worried that a friend may have an eating disorder, there are a few signs you can look out for.

Negative body image. Obsessing about body size or engaging in negative self-talk are early warning signs of the more common eating disorders like anorexia nervosa and bulimia nervosa.

Eating rituals. People with anorexia may spend time cutting their food in a certain way or

(continued on the next page)

(continued from the previous page)

pushing it around their plate. They may also eat only certain types of foods (those that are low in calories and fat).

Fear of eating in public. A person struggling with an eating disorder is more likely to shy away from eating in public because the experience can provoke anxiety.

Trips to the bathroom after eating. Frequent bathroom trips after meals may be a sign that a

Some people with eating disorders become obsessed with exercise, rarely missing a workout or panicking if they do.

person is purging—forcing themselves to throw up or abusing laxatives—after eating. Check for signs or smells of vomiting or the presence of packages of laxatives or diuretics.

Dressing in layers. Is your loved one wearing coats or heavy sweaters, even when it's hot? He may be trying to stay warm, attempting to hide his weight loss, or both.

Fine body hair. People who have starved their bodies of necessary nutrients over a period of time begin developing a soft layer of hair on their arms and legs. It's the body's way of defending itself against heat loss due to extreme weight loss.

Social withdrawal. Is your social butterfly friend suddenly avoiding regular activities? Anorexics experience drastic changes in their personalities. Some go from being happy and energetic to being listless and withdrawn.

Obsession with exercise. Sometimes referred to as "exercise anorexia," an obsession with exercise can coexist with an eating disorder. Warning signs include people panicking if they miss a workout or going to the gym even if they're sick or injured.

At twenty-three years old, Gerges said he was "finally confident and comfortable" in his skin.

Traumatic Events

A major disturbance such as physical or sexual abuse can sometimes serve as a catalyst for an eating disorder. Trauma survivors frequently struggle with feelings of guilt and a lack of control that may lead them to unhealthy coping mechanisms. People sometimes develop an eating disorder as a way of regaining control over the traumatic event. Other stressors could include the death of a loved one or another significant loss or an injury that's difficult to overcome.

According to therapist Judy Scheel, writing on the NEDA blog, an eating disorder serves as a way to distance oneself from uncomfortable feelings that the traumatic event may bring up, as well as a way to relieve them. "From an abuse perspective, the eating disorder is a clever, albeit destructive means to accomplish both distance and numbing as well as a means to relive the painful past events through a recreating of it through eating disorder symptomatology. In effect, the individual with an eating disorder assumes roles of both the victim and abuser." Scheel explained that the person diagnosed with the eating disorder is at the mercy of its symptoms—vomiting, starving, binge eating—but is also taking on the role of the abuser by doing harm to his or her own body.

Lisa Hamp, a survivor of the Virginia Tech massacre in 2007, which left thirty-three people dead, told the *Atlantic* that the traumatic events of that day eleven years prior left her with high anxiety when she's in public places and an eating disorder that developed shortly afterward. Hamp said:

> *My eating habits were changed, but I didn't understand the relationship at that time between my eating habits and the shooting. It was a slow development of an eating disorder. Virginia Tech didn't cause the eating disorder, but it was triggered by it. There were lots of seeds already planted, and Virginia Tech just started to grow them.*

There are other kinds of trauma that can trigger eating disorders as well. Researchers from the Joint Doctoral Program in Clinical Psychology at San Diego State University and the University of California–San Diego found that there is a relationship between eating disorders and sexual trauma. Being sexually assaulted can lead to body shame. In turn, body shame can lead to disordered eating.

Caroline Rothstein, an eating disorder and sexual assault survivor, penned an essay for *Marie Claire* in which she wrote, "Because I am a survivor of both rape and sexual abuse, my body has been—more than once—a crime scene. Throughout this time, I also struggled with depression, self-harm, and suicidal ideation. Now, at 34, I've been fully recovered from an eating disorder and self-harm for 13 years."

How to Cope with Triggers

According to the NEDA, different things may trigger a person's "eating disorder voice"—the internal dialogue that compels a person with disordered eating to continue negative behavior such as overeating, starving, bingeing and purging, and overexercising, to name a few. Triggers can be anything from billboard messages promoting thinness and diets to well-meaning friends or family members commenting on someone's weight, even if it's meant as a compliment. One way to cope with triggers is to develop an awareness of them.

Pay attention to triggers that come up during the day or the week and write a list of them. What are the thoughts

One way to cope with eating disorder triggers is to talk to a friend, especially if that person is not judgmental and can listen to what you have to say without telling you what to do.

and feelings that arise as a result of these triggers? How can the "healthy self" counteract the "eating disorder voice" for each of these triggers? Separating unhealthy thoughts from healthy ones is one useful technique.

No one should have to battle the "eating disorder voice" alone. Another effective practice is to develop and reach out to a support network. Whether it's a nutritionist, therapist, mentor, friend, family member, or significant other, it can be very effective to talk to someone when you're feeling triggered enough to engage in self-destructive actions. Not only are people from your support network there to listen, they can provide alternative coping mechanisms or suggest an activity to district you in that moment until the negative and anxious feelings subside. Engaging in self-care and practicing self-compassion are other approaches to combat that negative voice that creeps up when you are triggered. Instead of engaging in negative self-talk, it's important to treat yourself with the same kindness you would offer a friend who is experiencing a difficult moment. Suggestions for self-care include meditating, journaling, reading a book, going for a walk, making a gratitude list, or doing anything else that feels relaxing.

How to Help a Friend Who Has an Eating Disorder

If you have a friend or loved one who is suffering from an eating disorder, it can be hard to know what to do or say to help. Certain myths about eating disorders may cause well-meaning people to say something that can actually make the problem worse. Here are some suggestions for how you can help your loved one while also taking care of yourself.

Reject eating disorder myths. A person doesn't have to be dangerously thin to be anorexic or bulimic. Also, having an eating disorder is not a sign of being vain, narcissistic, or attention seeking. It is an illness that the person cannot control.

Don't use combative language. Psychologists recommend using "I" statements when talking to a person you're trying to help, since "you" statements can put that person on the defensive. For example, you can say, "I'm worried about your weight loss. How can I help?" instead of a more abrasive and less helpful, "You're out of control."

Forgo self-criticism. Avoid talking about your body—or anyone else's—in a negative way, especially if a friend or loved one is feeling sensitive about his or her body-image issues. For instance, don't talk about how you want to lose weight or how you're trying to eat less junk food.

Don't manipulate your friend into eating. Guilt-tripping or begging a friend to have a meal will not work, and it may further alienate him or her.

Be encouraging. Listen to what your friend says about what makes him or her feel out of control, and ask if there's any way you can help. Encourage your friend to find an activity—such as music, art, taking a walk, or reading—to help him or her deal with stress or emotional pain.

Remember, recovery isn't linear. Your friend may have been treated for his or her eating disorder and found healthy ways of coping with stress and triggers, but he or she may also relapse into old behaviors months or years after recovering. Exercise patience and compassion.

Set boundaries. Being a friend to someone with an eating disorder can be emotionally exhausting. Find time to take care of yourself and do something that you find relaxing.

Medical Care and Other Treatment

Some symptoms of eating disorders, such as significant weight loss that leads to malnutrition, can be life threatening. In these cases, the immediate goal is to ensure that the person is medically stable, so inpatient hospitalization may be necessary. Other times, people may be both medically and psychiatrically stable, but they would benefit from additional support to recover from unhealthy eating patterns and weight issues. Eating disorders can also frequently coexist with other illnesses like depression, substance abuse, or anxiety disorders. Medical professionals may take a holistic approach to treat coexisting disorders.

Inpatient Hospitalization

If a person's vital signs—blood pressure, pulse, respiration rate, and temperature—are unstable

People diagnosed with serious eating disorders may have to be admitted to a hospital until they are medically and psychologically stable.

and if lab findings indicate an acute health risk, a patient may be admitted to a hospital. Those physical criteria are often accompanied by psychiatric instability, including suicidal thoughts or rapidly worsening symptoms.

While in the hospital, patients receive twenty-four-hour-a-day medical attention, which may include daily weigh-ins and vital sign checks, meal monitoring, medication, group therapy meetings, and appointments with psychiatrists, dietitians, and other health professionals. If patients are unable to regain or maintain weight, they may receive medical refeeding, which involves having a nasogastric tube inserted from the nose to the stomach to supplement calorie intake and help them gain weight.

Molly Twomey, a contributor for the Mighty, describes her experience of inpatient treatment for anorexia: "Dinner takes two hours and then the bathrooms are locked ... Life is exhausting as an inpatient. I was forced to feel different emotions, come face to face with my disorder and recognize my real vulnerable self."

Since hospitalization is expensive, it is usually short term. When patients' vitals are stabilized, they are often moved to a partial hospitalization program (PHP) or a nonmedical treatment facility, where they continue to receive care and support.

My Struggle and Recovery from Anorexia Nervosa: The Author's Perspective

As a child, I happily ate second and third helpings of my Grandmother Juana's homemade Cuban rice and beans with shredded beef and fried plantains. Her food and unconditional love comforted me. At school, I was mercilessly bullied for being what was considered overweight.

When I was twelve, a bout of food poisoning caused me to lose 10 pounds and receive a lot of compliments from my peers, so I began to diet. Soon, I began obsessing over nutrition labels, cutting out all fat grams, and then eating only dinner. I'd insist that I eat alone or with my dog—Bingo's girth was expanding while my frame was shrinking.

The initial 10 pounds I shed soon became 20, 30, and then 40 pounds. I dropped down to a skeletal 60 pounds, and that was when my Cuban immigrant parents snapped out of their denial and realized I had an eating disorder.

I spent close to two years in emergency rooms and then in an eating disorder residential facility. At first, I was in culture shock because most of the other patients were white and affluent, and nobody else spoke Spanish, but I soon bonded with the other anorexic patients. Sometimes, bulimics and anorexics formed strategic alliances. Since mealtimes were monitored by staff, anorexics would sit with bulimics and pass food under the table to them. They could fulfill their need to binge, and we could get away with restricting our food intake. Once I realized these alliances were unhealthy, I knew I was on the path to recovery.

By the time I was seventeen, I had recovered from anorexia and learned healthier coping mechanisms, but my recovery has not been without challenges. A devastating breakup in 2005 and my grandmother's death in 2012 both led to significant bouts of weight loss. But my support team helped me get through these traumas without needing hospitalizations.

The author, Carmen Cusido, is shown here in Aruba in 2015. Cusido has been recovered from anorexia for years but sometimes still needs help coping with triggers.

Partial Hospitalization and Outpatient Treatments

Some people with eating disorders are medically stable, but their eating disorder may still impair their functioning, and they may still need daily assessments of their mental and physiological status. A psychiatric assessment may show that a person engages in daily binge eating, purging, limiting food intake, fasting, or other methods to control his or her weight.

Specialized eating disorder facilities may offer PHPs, which give individuals the structure and intensity of a full-time residential program but allow them and their loved ones to continue to practice recovery skills at home. PHPs may include a combination of individual, group, and family therapy sessions that focus on recovery skills and the role families play in lasting recovery.

Outpatient programs—along with medication, if necessary—may help people continue on a path to recovery.

Treatment facilities offer outpatient treatment including group therapy and partial hospitalization programs for people diagnosed with eating disorders.

59

While some prefer individualized one-on-one sessions with therapists and other professionals, like nutritionists, others may opt to attend weekly or monthly self-help groups to keep them from relapsing into their eating disorders.

At a hospital in Lawrence, Kansas, which offers inpatient and outpatient treatments, people are weighed each morning and get their blood pressure and pulses taken. Once a week, patients at McCallum Place and its sister location, Menorah Medical Center, have their blood drawn and their temperature taken to ensure their health is maintained. Patients also work with therapists, psychiatrists, and dietitians to learn about everything from the harmful effects of starvation to facing their "fear foods" (the foods they believe will make them gain weight rapidly). "We don't see our bodies the way other people do," said eighteen-year-old Zoe Prather, who entered treatment at McCallum Place during her junior year of high school. "When I was at 100 pounds, I thought that I looked like I weighed 200. I didn't understand why my clothes didn't fit because I looked like I'd gained weight instead of lost it."

Maddy Fowler, a student at the University of Buffalo, started her path to recovery from an EDNOS after entering a PHP. "For all its trials and tribulations, stresses, failures, anxiety and heartbreak, I would take real life and recovery over my eating disorder any day," Fowler wrote for the university's newspaper, the *Spectrum*. "Because recovery lets you see Taylor Swift live with your best friends instead of listening to her CDs in your hospital room. Recovery lets you eat brownies without tears. Recovery is dancing the night away without getting dizzy."

Choosing the Right Treatment

Medical treatments vary, depending on the type and severity of the eating disorder. However, because eating disorders go beyond a person's relationship with food, it is important to take a holistic approach when it comes to treatment. According to the National Institute of Mental Health, treatment options include individual, group, or family psychotherapy; medical care and monitoring; nutritional counseling; and medications.

The first step is to visit a mental health professional or primary care doctor, who may recommend a team of professionals who specialize in the treatment of eating disorders. They may include a psychologist or psychiatrist who can provide medication; a registered dietitian to give counseling on meal planning and nutrition; medical or dental specialists to treat health problems that result from an eating disorder; and family members, parents, or partners to supervise meals and support the patient throughout the treatment process.

A treatment team can recommend plans (such as hospitalization or outpatient treatment), address financial concerns, and set goals to help the patient achieve a healthy weight, normalize eating patterns,

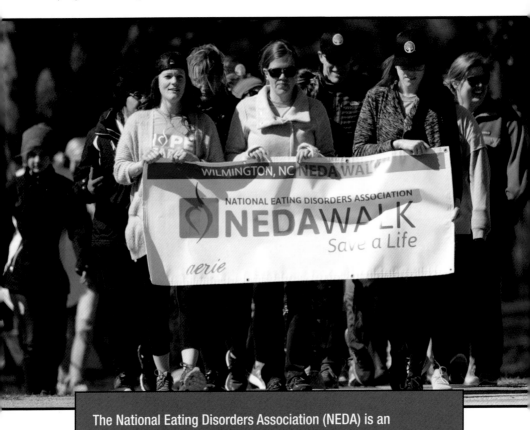

The National Eating Disorders Association (NEDA) is an organization that raises awareness of these mental illnesses and their impacts.

and develop positive ways to cope with stress and negative emotions.

Types of Psychotherapy

Psychotherapy is the treatment of mental health issues, including eating disorders, using psychological rather than medical techniques. Psychotherapy helps people take control of their lives and respond to stress and challenges with healthy coping skills. Treatment typically involves talking to psychiatrists, psychologists, or other mental health professionals. The following are a number of different approaches to help treat eating disorders.

Cognitive Behavioral Therapy

A therapist using cognitive behavioral therapy (CBT) teaches participants skills to help them identify problematic beliefs and negative patterns and offers them healthy ways to cope with emotions. CBT helps patients address psychological, societal, and familial factors that may have contributed to their eating disorder.

For India Benjamin, an English woman with a history of anorexia and depression, "working through the [CBT] exercises helped me to identify how irrational thought patterns influenced my mood and behaviour, and taught me ways to work around and tackle these problematic thought patterns." According to psychotherapist Geraldine Joaquim, therapies like CBT "help to train the brain to focus on the positives, which not only equips you to deal with triggers and events, but affects a chemical change in the brain, which can help to rebalance the hormones that play a part in depression."

Acceptance and Commitment Therapy

Acceptance and commitment therapy (ACT) helps individuals focus on changing their actions rather than their thoughts and feelings. This approach also teaches participants that pain and anxiety are common life stressors and encourages them to detach themselves from these emotions.

Emily Sandoz, a psychologist, faculty member at the University of Louisiana–Lafayette, and coauthor of *Acceptance and Commitment Therapy for Eating Disorders*, explained why she has embraced ACT. "Traditional CBT says that when our thoughts are better, when they're more accurate and less distressing, then our behavior will be better and we'll be more effective in our lives. A traditional CBT approach would say you need to think positively. In ACT, we would say: 'Who cares what you think? Can you pursue effective behavior and a meaningful life no matter what's going on in your head?' That's the main difference."

Using ACT to approach eating disorders and body-image issues works by teaching subjects how to learn effective living skills to handle distress, Sandoz said. "In ACT, what's unique is we link acceptance to living a meaningful life." Sandoz typically asks subjects questions like, "Would you be willing to have these terrible thoughts and feelings about your body if it meant you're able to live the life you want to live? … If it meant you could be more active in your community?"

She said ACT helps patients evaluate what they really care about.

Art Therapy

A professional using this form of psychotherapy often guides patients to use painting, pottery making, drawing, and sculpting to illustrate their feelings, thoughts, and personal stories. Art therapy provides a creative outlet for people who suffer from eating

Some people with eating disorders use art therapy—sculpting, drawing, painting, or other mediums—to express their feelings about their illnesses or their triggers.

disorders, and it can be useful for treating coexisting disorders, such as substance abuse or mood disorders.

Candy Ward, a ceramicist living in London, uses art to help manage her eating disorder. "I'm finding art psychotherapy really helpful as I'm able to express myself in a way that words sometimes can't."

After developing bulimia as a teenager after years of extreme dieting, Jenna Rose Simon took to drawing to help her depict her struggle with an eating disorder. The sketches she made in art therapy turned into her book *Unbroken: An Art Book; My Journey So Far, Plus 20 Feel-Good Drawing Activities*, which includes space at the end of each chapter for subjects to draw for themselves. "I'm definitely still in progress. I don't always feel great in my own skin, and I do pay some attention to what I eat," Simon said in an interview with CNN in April 2017.

Dialectical Behavioral Therapy

Dialectical behavioral therapy (DBT) helps people cope with painful emotional circumstances and extreme behaviors. This type of psychotherapy focuses on emotional regulation and mindfulness. Originally designed for people diagnosed with borderline personality disorder, DBT can help those with eating disorders because it paves the way for individuals to gain control over negative emotions and thoughts and better deal with stressful situations.

"Dialectical Behavior Therapy has been shown to be quite effective for people struggling with bulimia and binge eating disorders," according to Dr. Ellen Astrachan-Fletcher in a blog post for the Eating Recovery Center website. "People with these issues

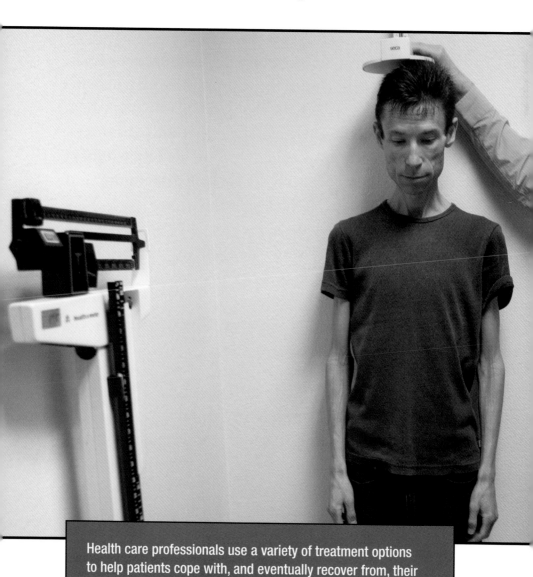

Health care professionals use a variety of treatment options to help patients cope with, and eventually recover from, their eating disorders.

tend to be emotionally under-controlled, struggling with high sensitivity, high reactivity and a slow return to baseline." Patients with anorexia, who tend to be more "emotionally over-controlled," may benefit from radically open DBT, which helps individuals increase traits like adaptability, receptivity and intimacy, and connectedness.

The primary objective of DBT is to help a person create a life "they want to be present in," Astrachan-Fletcher wrote. "When this goal is accomplished, target behaviors (including eating disorders, substance abuse, suicidal ideation and self-injury) will no longer be used to escape discomfort and emotional pain." Through DBT, patients may learn to coexist with uncomfortable emotions, be present in the moment, use skills to accept life as it is, and learn how to decrease intense emotions.

Exposure and Response Prevention Therapy

Typically used to treat obsessive-compulsive disorder, exposure and response prevention therapy (ERP) can also be effective in treating eating disorders because it helps individuals by exposing them to what they're afraid of. It helps them overcome their fears of eating certain foods and decreases their urge to binge and purge.

Laura Lange, the director of the Binge Eating Treatment and Recovery Program at the Eating Recovery Center in Illinois, said ERP therapists help patients "understand how they may overestimate how awful their affective (emotional) experiences will be" and "understand how they may underestimate their ability to cope with their experiences," among other therapeutic goals. This treatment approach allows patients to guide their own treatment and take control of their recovery.

Patients with eating disorders could find ERP useful because they're learning to practice skills in a controlled setting while also being exposed to triggers that may have fueled their eating disorders in the first place. "ERP is used to target and decrease fear of feeling negative emotions and the avoidance that results when patients fear feeling uncomfortable," said Lange.

Family-Based Therapy

Also known as the Maudsley method, family-based therapy (FBT) was developed as an alternative to traditional forms of intervention—including hospitalization. This approach actively engages parents in their child's recovery process from eating disorders, empowering them to help their child return to a healthy weight at home. According to Daniel Le Grange, director of the eating disorders program at the University of Chicago, "With just

The Maudsley method, also known as family-based therapy, actively engages parents in their child's recovery process, empowering them to help the child at home.

about every other illness, psychiatric or medical, parents are always seen as a resource to help kids. With anorexia treatment, for some reason, we have excluded parents. This treatment [FBT] is telling parents, 'You can do this.'"

During phase one of this treatment, parents take complete control over what their child eats, just as a professional might do in an inpatient treatment program. In phase two, parents begin to hand control of food intake back to their child. Phase three focuses on long-term strategies to help manage the illness.

However, critics of the treatment question the long-term effectiveness of this approach and whether it works for people who are severely malnourished. "When patients are losing weight rapidly, it's rare to be able to turn it around, and they often must move to a higher level of care," like hospitalization or residential treatment, according to Michael Strober, director of the eating disorders program at the University of California–Los Angeles, in a 2010 interview with the *New York Times*.

CHAPTER FOUR

Recovery and Relapse

Recovery from eating disorders is complicated, but it is not impossible. There is little data on how many individuals ultimately recover from these mental health illnesses, and there's no set timeline for recovery. It can take months or even years before someone develops or relearns healthy eating habits and behaviors.

However, psychologists have identified three broad areas of recovery: physical, behavioral, and psychological. Those struggling with eating disorders must address their immediate medical needs first—which may include gaining weight, normalizing hormone levels and electrolytes, and resuming menstruation. After individuals are medically and psychiatrically stabilized, they may remain under outpatient care in order to continue relearning healthy eating habits and coping skills.

It is common for a person to relapse after recovering from an eating disorder. Some people are triggered into relapsing when they get pregnant or give birth.

But along the way, relapses are common. Some stressors that can lead to a relapse include major life events such as going off to college, starting a new job, moving away from home or to a new town, getting married or divorced, giving birth, the death of a loved one, or the diagnosis of a chronic illness.

Some people choose to say they are "recovering" rather than "recovered" because the process is not linear. In a featured Humans of New York post from September 2017, a woman revealed she began purging in October 2013 as a college freshman, and it became progressively worse over the next five months. The interviewee, who was not named, said she began to regain control when she began taking about it. "The eating disorder lost its power when it stopped being a secret," she said. Though she had had a recent relapse at the time she was interviewed, she said she reminded herself that it didn't erase the progress she had made over the years.

For others, recovery is more elusive, and relapse can happen years after the initial onset of the disorder. Dr. Suzanne Dooley-Hash has had anorexia for more than thirty years, and she doubts she will ever recover from it. During a relapse in 2005, she lost a dangerous amount of weight in six months and had to take a nineteen-month hiatus from her job as an emergency room physician so she could focus on her health. "I'm a physician at a really high-powered institution, and I've published in well-respected journals—I'm functional. I don't think functionality is necessarily a good measure," Dooley-Hash said in a 2001 interview with the *New York Times*.

However, there are plenty of stories of those who survive and thrive, even after years of living with

It is possible to recover from an eating disorder, but it takes courage and resilience. It's important to be aware of your eating disorder triggers and to manage them carefully.

an eating disorder. In a 2015 article on BuzzFeed, a number of eating disorder survivors shared their recovery stories. "Every meal, I choose to eat and eat well. If I have to do this for the rest of my life, so be it. Recovery is not an easy path, but it is the right one, and the one that takes the most strength to walk down," said Ben Carter. In the same article, June Alexander defined recovery as something that "requires a lot of courage; and for best results, to maintain recovery, it requires openness and acceptance in a village of people who understand and who care."

For Canada-based writer Olivia Robinson, her recovery from bulimia wasn't a "picture-perfect success story." She is critical of the fact that specific conversations about eating disorders move "at a snail's pace," though conversations about mental health illnesses have progressed. "We speak in platitudes about the 'road to recovery' with eating disorders, like there's an easily replicable strategy, like winning a board game. My recovery was a hellish game of snakes and ladders: I'd make progress and then have a setback and slide back to start," Robinson recounted in the Huffington Post in 2017. When she wrote this, it had been nearly seven years since her first bulimic episode. "My recovery wasn't smooth, but eventually, I came up for air. Even now it's not easy, but I know my triggers and possess the ability to cope and deflect my symptoms."

Actress Lily Collins, who has been in recovery for years, was afraid she'd relapse into her eating disorder after portraying a young woman with a similar illness in the Netflix film *To the Bone*. "I was terrified that doing the movie would take me backward, but I had to remind myself that they hired me to tell a story, not to

Actress Lily Collins was worried that she might relapse into her eating disorder when she had to lose weight for her role in *To the Bone*, a movie about a woman with anorexia.

be a certain weight," she said. "In the end, it was a gift to be able to step back into shoes I had once worn but from a mature place." Collins has also written a book, *Unfiltered*, about her experience with eating disorders. "Having suffered from an eating disorder doesn't define me; I'm not ashamed of my past," she said.

Living with Someone Who Has an Eating Disorder

Parents and significant others of people with eating disorders may question their role in the development and recovery of the disorder, wondering if something they did or said led to the disorder. One important thing to remember is that eating disorders do not arise from one particular event or situation, according to Merryl Bear at the Canada-based National Eating Disorder Information Centre (NEDIC). There are often a series of factors—including a person's coping style and personality—that can serve as a catalyst for the disorder.

Neither the people with eating disorders nor their family members are to blame for the eating disorder. The enemy is the eating disorder itself. Bear recommends that loved ones of people with eating disorders educate themselves about the illness and refrain from focusing on the person's weight and food intake. Ultimately, the people with the eating disorders have to take responsibility for their own recovery processes.

The NEDIC suggests the following survival strategies for families of loved ones with an eating disorder: realizing that there's no easy fix to the illness, attending support groups, encouraging the person with the eating disorder to seek help, showing support and compassion, expressing love—physically and verbally—for the person, helping the person learn to value himself or herself, setting appropriate expectations for the person, engaging with the person on issues other than food and weight, and maintaining a positive attitude.

Writing on Everyday Feminism, Kaila Prins recommends a number of ways to be an ally while a partner is in the process of recovering from an eating disorder. One of those ways is to recognize that eating disorders are mental illnesses. Making judgments and offering unsolicited advice doesn't help. What does help is giving the person space and support. It is also important to be aware of your language and how it could trigger a person with an eating disorder. Casually mentioning diets, workouts, or your weight could encourage someone to engage in unhealthy eating behaviors.

One thing to avoid is trying to "fix" a loved one's eating disorder, according to Leora Fulvio, a licensed psychotherapist and certified clinical hypnotherapist

It's important to support a loved one with an eating disorder, but don't try to "fix" him or her because that could lead to a codependent relationship.

specializing in the treatment of eating disorders. Attempting to fix the disorder creates codependency in the relationship and may make the eating disorder worse. At the same time, it is important to encourage the individual to get treatment. Also, remember not to mention your loved one's appearance, and don't talk about his or her food. If the person asks whether he or she "looks fat in these jeans," Fulvio suggests responding by mentioning how much you love him or her.

How to Maintain Recovery

After years of unhealthy eating behaviors and negative coping mechanisms, what could a life in recovery look like? Here are some tips on how to begin or continue the journey toward recovering from an eating disorder.

Set small goals. Work on small goals that gradually lead to bigger ones. For example, is it difficult to eat out? Practice eating with loved ones at home first. Once you've achieved that goal, it may be time to set the next one, which could include eating out at a restaurant.

(continued on the next page)

(continued from the previous page)

Eschew the comfort zone. Steps toward recovery may be uncomfortable and may include going through physical changes and working through painful emotions. But with consistency and time, what was once uncomfortable—getting to a healthy weight, eating fear foods, monitoring food intake by establishing a meal plan—will become part of your new everyday routine.

Summon support. Reach out to loved ones or members of your medical team if you're struggling and need some help.

What to Do If You Relapse

One vital part of maintaining recovery from an eating disorder is having a strong support system. However, even with continued treatment and loving family and friends, people can still fall back into disordered thinking and eating patterns. There are a few warning signs of a potential relapse. These include taking a longer time to finish eating, becoming more irritable, exercising in secret, and unexpected weight changes. But there are also actions you can take to continue your path to recovery.

Seek help from a professional immediately. Quick action is key to returning to healthy eating patterns and behaviors.

Make yourself accountable. One action—such as intentionally skipping a meal, overeating, or bingeing and purging—should not be an excuse to continue other disordered behaviors. One strategy is to schedule a meal plan and stick to it.

List the benefits of recovery. Are there life goals, such as traveling abroad, that you can only accomplish if you're healthy? Write those down for inspiration!

Be aware of triggers. Are there places, events, or people that make you feel anxious? How do you cope with that? Write down what works and what doesn't.

Use mantras. Look up inspirational quotes or mantras to keep you motivated.

Focus on "me time." Take a walk, do yoga, read a book, light a candle, or find some other way to relax when you're stressed. If you feel like you may resort to old, negative habits and behaviors, destressing can help the feeling pass.

Forgive yourself. It may have taken months or years for your eating disorder to develop. Recovery could similarly take a long time, and there may be setbacks along the way. It's important not to dwell on them.

Keep track of your progress. It may seem like you still have a long way to go, but don't forget how far you've already come.

Overcoming Eating Disorders: Recovery Stories

Karla Mosley, an actress and producer living in Los Angeles, received unhealthy messages about her body at a young age. As a black girl in an area that was predominantly white, she began feeling something was "wrong" with her body in high school, where "the standard of beauty around me was literally impossible for me to achieve. And while I knew I'd never be blond or white, as my thighs grew bigger,

One way to start or continue a journey toward recovery is to keep track of the progress you've made, whether it's recognizing a trigger, eating a "fear food," or another accomplishment.

my hips curved, and my butt and stomach rounded, I felt I could—or should—control that," she said in an interview with *Glamour*.

Mosley binged and purged for years until her employer found out in 2003 and gave her an ultimatum: get help or leave the show she was on at the time. "I had to learn to challenge beliefs that I didn't know were disordered because they had been with me for so long," Mosley told *Glamour*. "And I'm still untangling those backward beliefs that I probably made up when I was 10 years old." Years after her struggle began, Mosley said she came to the realization that her family, fans, friends, and others don't love her because of her dress size or, she added jokingly, her love of hip-hop. "They love me because of the essence of me. Beauty comes from inside."

For twenty-eight-year-old Mike Marjama, a Seattle Mariners catcher, his eating disorder and resulting hospitalization briefly prevented him from playing his beloved baseball during his junior year in high school. During the eighth grade, he began restricting his diet and overexercising. "I put a stationary bike in the shower, and [would] ride until I would pass out," he said in an ABC News interview. Marjama first struggled with anorexia but then turned to bingeing and purging and bulimia. After entering an inpatient program for five days during the eleventh grade, Marjama said he realized he was a threat to himself and became aware of his illness.

Actress Karla Mosley, who is now recovered from an eating disorder, said she received unhealthy messages about her body at a young age.

Now in recovery, Marjama is detailing his struggle with eating disorders in a new documentary for Uninterrupted, a multimedia platform for athletes. "If I can maybe affect one person that doesn't have to have their hopes and dreams taken away from them because they're suffering from an eating disorder, and they're able to follow their hopes and dreams, that's all I really want," he said.

Micaela Evans also shatters the stereotype that eating disorders primarily affect thin, white, able-bodied women. In a piece for Teen Vogue, Evans, who has a disability and has used a wheelchair since she was two, recounted how restricting her eating to "dangerous levels" left her physical health "spiraling downwards." Body-image issues at fourteen turned into an eating disorder, but as she sought help for it, she was dismissed by a few medical professionals. "As a disabled woman, I didn't fit the narrowly defined expectations of

As a teen, Mike Marjama of the Seattle Mariners was briefly hospitalized for an eating disorder after he began overexercising and restricting his food intake.

what someone's body 'should be like' and it seemed to baffle doctors who were not accustomed to supporting individuals like me."

In her determination to overcome the illness, Evans sought help from friends and family. The Canadian college student—who, despite some struggles, said she is "fully in recovery"—stressed to others who have disabilities and are dealing with an eating disorder that they are not alone, and "it is possible to get better, no matter what your body looks like or how it moves through this world."

Kristina Saffran and Liana Rosenman first met at age thirteen while undergoing treatment for their eating disorders. After they reached recovery, Saffran and Rosenman wanted to help others with eating disorders do the same. At age fifteen, they founded Project HEAL, a nonprofit dedicated to helping people with eating disorders afford treatment, which can cost up to $30,000 per month. It has become the second-largest eating disorder nonprofit in the United States, with forty chapters worldwide and partnerships with treatment centers across the nation, according to *Forbes*.

"We were really lucky in that our insurance paid for most of our treatment, and our parents could pay the rest," Saffran said in a 2012 interview with *People*. "But we saw people who really wanted it and couldn't afford it and ended up relapsing. So one day, we were talking, sort of idealistically, and we said, 'We should do something,' and we planned our first fundraiser." They've since raised hundreds of thousands of dollars to help people with eating disorders get the treatment they need.

If you or someone you love is in the grips of an eating disorder, it may seem as if there is no hope. But as these recovery stories illustrate, with the right treatment and support, it is possible to overcome an eating disorder and go on to have a bright future.

10 Great Questions to Ask a Specialist

1. I think my friend or family member has an eating disorder. What should I do?

2. How long have you been treating eating disorders and what are your credentials?

3. Do I need a medical evaluation before entering the treatment program?

4. How much does this treatment cost? Will my insurance reimburse me for part of the treatment?

5. What should I expect during a therapy session? What kind of approach will you use to help me achieve my goal of overcoming my eating disorder?

6. What medical services do you provide? How do you manage medical complications that arise with eating disorders or co-occurring psychiatric conditions such as depression?

7. What is my target weight? How will you help me achieve it?

8. Who are the members of my treatment team, and how do you all collaborate?

9. What themes will be covered in my therapy sessions?

10. What is the average length of stay for this program?

acceptance and commitment therapy (ACT) An approach that helps individuals focus on changing their actions rather than their thoughts and feelings.

anorexia nervosa An eating disorder characterized by a pathological fear of weight gain that leads to excessive weight loss, malnutrition, and unhealthy eating patterns. Physical characteristics may include the stoppage of menstrual periods, loss of calcium that leads to thinning bones, brittle hair and nails, drop in body temperature, and depression and lethargy.

art therapy Therapy that involves using a creative outlet like drawing, sculpting, painting, or pottery making to illustrate feelings, thoughts, and personal stories to help with the healing process.

avoidant/restrictive food intake disorder (ARFID) An eating disorder characterized by failing to meet daily nutritional requirements because of a lack of interest in eating or the avoidance of food with certain characteristics, such as color, texture, smell, or taste. Unlike with anorexia nervosa, a person with ARFID is not avoiding food because of fear of gaining weight.

binge eating disorder (BED) An eating disorder characterized by frequent episodes of eating large quantities of food, followed by a sense of lack of control.

bulimia nervosa An eating disorder characterized by compulsive overeating, usually followed by self-induced vomiting or the abuse of laxatives and diuretics. Some symptoms of the illness include a chronically inflamed and sore throat.

cognitive behavioral therapy (CBT) A common type of talk therapy used both to manage and prevent a relapse of mental illness symptoms. This approach may help a person identify ways to manage emotions and learn better ways to communicate.

dialectical behavioral therapy (DBT) A common type of talk therapy that helps individuals learn to manage emotions that feel uncomfortable and reduce impulsiveness by observing feelings rather than acting on them.

eating disorders Psychological disorders characterized by serious disturbances of eating behaviors.

exposure and response prevention therapy (ERP) Typically used to treat individuals with obsessive-compulsive disorder, ERP can also be effective in treating eating disorders because it helps people overcome their fears of eating certain foods and decreases their urge to binge and purge.

family-based therapy (FBT) An intensive outpatient therapy with a primary goal of avoiding hospitalization. With FBT, parents are responsible for restoring their child to a healthy weight at home. FBT is also known as the Maudsley method.

fear food Certain kinds of food or certain quantities of food that a person fears will lead to noticeable and instant weight gain. Those foods could include food like desserts, meat, or any other high-calorie item.

inpatient hospitalization Twenty-four-hour-a-day treatment provided in a hospital.

mental health illness A wide range of disorders that affect a person's mood, thinking, and behavior. Examples of mental health illnesses include eating disorders, depression, and anxiety disorders.

partial hospitalization Continued care for an individual with an eating disorder who may be medically stable but whose eating disorder may still impair daily functioning. The person may receive the structure and intensity of a full-time residential program while continuing to practice recovery skills at home.

pica An uncommon eating disorder characterized by a desire to eat nonfood items like chalk, sand, hair, and other substances that have no nutritional value.

purging Forcing oneself to vomit after eating a lot of food to avoid gaining weight.

recovery The process of combating a disorder or a real or perceived problem.

relapse To fall back or regress into unhealthy patterns after making progress toward recovery

rumination syndrome An uncommon eating disorder characterized by repeatedly but unintentionally spitting up undigested or partially digested food. The person then rechews the food and either reswallows it or spits it out.

social withdrawal The avoidance of people and activities one would usually enjoy.

trigger A person, place, event, incident, or emotion that sets off unhealthy feelings or behaviors.

American Psychiatric Association (APA)
800 Maine Avenue SW, Suite 900
Washington DC 20024
(888) 357-7924 or (888) 357-7924
Website: https://www.psychiatry.org
Facebook: @AmericanPsychiatricAssociation
Instagram and Twitter: @APAPsychiatric
The APA is an organization of psychiatrists working
to ensure effective and humane treatment for
all people with mental illness. A hallmark of
its mission is to promote psychiatric education
and research while advocating for patients.

Binge Eating Disorder Association (BEDA)
637 Emerson Place
Severna Park, MD 21146
(855) 855-2332 (toll free)
Website: https://bedaonline.com
Facebook: @BEDAonline
Twitter: @BEDAorg
A national organization founded in 2008, the
BEDA focuses on providing recognition,
prevention, and treatment for binge
eating disorder and the stigma associated
with this specific eating disorder.

National Alliance on Mental Illness (NAMI)
3803 N. Fairfax Drive, Suite 100

Arlington, VA 22203

(800) 950-6264

Website: https://www.nami.org

Facebook: @NAMI

Instagram and Twitter: @NAMICommunicate

A grassroots mental health organization dedicated to building better lives for the millions affected by mental illness, NAMI focuses on educating families, individuals, and educators; shaping public policies for people with mental illness; providing free referral, information, and support; and leading public awareness events and activities.

National Association of Anorexia Nervosa and Associated Disorders (ANAD)

220 N. Green Street

Chicago, IL 60607

(630) 577-1330

Website: http://www.anad.org

Facebook: @ANADHelp

Instagram: @anadhelp

Twitter: @ANADSupport

As the oldest organization fighting eating disorders in the United States, ANAD provides resources for schools, families, and the eating disorder community.

National Eating Disorder Information Centre
  (NEDIC)
200 Elizabeth Street
Toronto, ON M5G 2C4
Canada
(866) 633-4220 and (416) 340-4156
Website: http://nedic.ca
Facebook: @thenedic
Instagram: @the_nedic
Twitter: @theNEDIC
The NEDIC operates a national toll-free help line
  for people with eating disorders. In addition,
  the organization focuses on awareness and
  prevention of eating disorders, disseminates
  information and resources, and delivers
  workshops, presentations, panel discussions,
  and webinars for different audiences.

National Eating Disorders Association (NEDA)
200 W. Forty-First Street, Suite 1203
New York, NY 10036
(800) 931-2237
Website: https://www.nationaleatingdisorders.org
Facebook: @NationalEatingDisordersAssociation
Instagram: @neda
Twitter: @NEDAstaff
As the largest nonprofit in the United States
  dedicated to supporting individuals affected by

eating disorders and their families, the NEDA provides a community of support in the fight against eating disorders.

National Initiative for Eating Disorders (NIED)
(647) 347-2393 or (416) 483-0956
Website: http://nied.ca
Facebook and Twitter: @niedcanada
Launched in 2012, the NIED strives to create awareness and action by offering free educational symposia presented by experts who include psychiatrists and nutritionists.

For Further Reading

Costin, Carolyn, and Gwen Schubert Grabb. *8 Keys to Recovery from an Eating Disorder.* New York, NY: W. W. Norton & Company, 2013.

Drew, Ursula, and Stephanie Watson. *Conquering Bulimia.* New York, NY: Rosen YA, 2016.

Dunkle, Elena, and Clare B. Dunkle. *Elena Vanishing: A Memoir.* San Francisco, CA: Chronicle Books, 2016.

Foran, Racquel. *Living with Eating Disorders.* North Mankato, MN: ABDO Publishing Company, 2014.

Haston, Meg. *Paperweight.* New York, NY: HarperTeen, 2017.

Landau, Jennifer. *Teens Talk About Body Image and Eating Disorders.* New York, NY: Rosen YA, 2018.

Lew, Kristi. *I Have an Eating Disorder. Now What?* New York, NY: Rosen YA, 2015.

Medoff, Jillian. *Hunger Point.* New York, NY: Harper Perennial, 2017.

Moskowitz, Hannah. *Not Otherwise Specified.* New York, NY: Simon Pulse, 2015.

Nardo, Don. *Teens and Eating Disorders.* San Diego, CA: ReferencePoint Press Inc., 2017.

Parys, Sabrina. *Helping a Friend with an Eating Disorder.* New York, NY: Rosen YA, 2017.

Schab, Lisa M. *The Bulimia Workbook for Teens: Activities to Help You Stop Bingeing and Purging.* Oakland, CA: New Harbinger Publications, 2011.

Tucker, Nancy. *The Time in Between: A Memoir of Hunger and Hope.* London, UK: Icon Books, 2016.

Wachter, Andrea. *Getting Over Overeating for Teens: A Workbook to Transfer Your Relationship with Food using CBT, Mindfulness, and Intuitive Eating.* Oakland, CA: New Harbinger Publications, 2016.

Watson, Stephanie. *Conquering Binge Eating.* New York, NY: Rosen YA, 2016.

Bibliography

Armstrong, Megan. "The 10 Most Honest Confessions from Demi Lovato's 'Simply Complicated' YouTube Documentary." *Billboard*, October 18, 2017. https://www.billboard.com /articles/columns/pop/8005791/demi-lovato -simply-complicated-documentary-youtube -best-moments.

BBC. "Bulimia Brains 'Use Food to Avoid Negative Thoughts.'" July 11, 2017. http://www.bbc.com /news/health-40556922.

Chamorro-Premuzic, Tomas. "Are Eating Disorders Heritable?" *Psychology Today*, April 8, 2012. https://www.psychologytoday.com/us/blog /mr-personality/201204/are-eating-disorders -heritable.

Crawford, Steven F., and Harry A. Brandt. "30 Million People Will Experience Eating Disorders—the CDC Needs to Help." The Hill, February 15, 2018. http://thehill.com/opinion/healthcare/374127 -30-million-people-will-experience-eating -disorders-the-cdc-needs-to-help.

Cusido, Carmen. "'Eat Up': How Cultural Messages Can Lead to Eating Disorders." NPR, December 7, 2015. https://www.npr.org /sections/thesalt/2015/12/07/458490852/eat -up-how-cultural-messages-can-lead-to -eating-disorders.

Daily Mail (London). "'It Wasn't About Body Image': Candace Cameron Bure Reveals Her Bulimia Stemmed from 'Losing Her Identity' When She Got Married." May 4, 2016. http://www.dailymail .co.uk/tvshowbiz/article-3573991/Candace -Cameron-Bure-opens-struggle-Bulimia-says -started-lonely.html#ixzz5AKSkRLY5.

Davenport, Nicole. "10 Ways to Cope with a Relapse in Eating Disorder Recovery." National Eating Disorders Association, July 2017. https://www .nationaleatingdisorders.org/blog/10-ways -cope-with-relapse-eating-disorder-recovery.

Eating Disorder Hope. "Anorexia Nervosa: Causes, Symptoms, Signs, and Treatment Help." Eating Disorder Education and Awareness. Retrieved April 29, 2018. https://www.eatingdisorderhope .com/information/anorexia.

Ellin, Abby. "In Fighting Anorexia, Recovery Is Elusive." *New York Times*, April 25, 2011. http://www.nytimes.com/2011/04/26/health /26anorexia.html.

Gleissner, Greta. "Social Media and Its Effect on Eating Disorders." Huffington Post, May 10, 2017. https://www.huffingtonpost.com /entry/social-media-and-its-effect-on-eating -disorders_us_591343bce4b0e3bb894d5caa.

Gomez, Patrick. "Good Morning America's Ginger Zee on How Her Family Helped Her Battle Anorexia as a Teen." *People*, June 22, 2016.

http://people.com/tv/ginger-zee-dancing-with-the-stars-good-morning-america-star-on-anorexia.

Jacoby, Sarah. "This Is Why It's So Complicated to Recover from an Eating Disorder." *SELF*, September 13, 2017. https://www.self.com/story/why-its-so-complicated-to-recover-from-an-eating-disorder.

Kirby, John, and Meagan McDowell. "Surviving and Thriving After a 6-Year Battle with an Eating Disorder." CNN, February 25, 2018. https://www.cnn.com/2018/02/23/opinions/dads-daughters-eating-disorders-kirby-and-mcdowell-opinion/index.html.

National Eating Disorders Association. "What Are Eating Disorders?" Retrieved May 15, 2018. https://www.nationaleatingdisorders.org/what-are-eating-disorders.

Pearson, Catherine. "Maudsley Method for Anorexia Treatment Puts Parents in Control of Their Child's Recovery." Huffington Post, September 19, 2013. https://www.huffingtonpost.com/2013/09/19/maudsley-method_n_3874816.html.

Petter, Olivia. "Worrying Increase in Promotion of Anorexia on Social Media Sites, New Study Finds." *Independent* (London), October 15, 2017. https://www.independent.co.uk/life-style/anorexia-social-media-bonespiration

-thinspo-bullimia-eating-disorder-instagram
-twitter-a8000461.html.

Praderio, Caroline. "Demi Lovato Shared Powerful Side-by-Side Photos to Document Her Eating Disorder Recovery." Insider, October 20, 2017. http://www.thisisinsider.com/demi-lovatos -eating-disorder-recovery-photos-2017-10.

Rojas, Marcela. "Social Media Helps Fuel Some Eating Disorders." *USA Today*, June 1, 2014. https://www.usatoday.com/story/news /nation/2014/06/01/social-media-helps-fuel -eating-disorders/9817513.

Ross, Ashley. "How America's Diet Culture Hinders Those with Eating Disorders." Daily Beast, January 10, 2018. https://www.thedailybeast .com/how-americas-diet-culture-hinders -those-with-eating-disorders.

Rothstein, Caroline. "17 Stories of Eating-Disorder Survival." BuzzFeed, February 24, 2015. https://www.buzzfeed.com/carolinerothstein /17-stories-of-eating-disorder-survival?utm _term=.bnZNX0ERD#.pom0anMvO.

Seemayer, Zach. "Exclusive: Candace Cameron Bure Talks Past Struggle with Bulimia: 'I Kind of Lost My Identity.'" *ET*, May 3, 2016. http:// www.etonline.com/news/188036_candace _cameron_bure_talks_past_struggle_with _bulimia.

Young, Sarah. "A Woman with Severe Anorexia Was Given Weeks to Live, but She Documented Her Incredible Recovery on Instagram." Business Insider, February 8, 2018. http://www .businessinsider.com/woman-with-anorexia -documented-recovery-on-instagram-2018 -2?r=UK&IR=T.

Zickel, Danielle. "What to Know About the Eating Disorder That Makes People Swallow Sharp Metal Objects." Men's Health, November 29, 2018. https://www.menshealth.com/health/pica -eating-disorder.

Index

About the Author

Carmen Cusido is a writer and a recovered anorexic. In addition to writing *Coping with Eating Disorders*, Cusido has authored articles and personal essays about eating disorders and mental health issues in communities of color for various outlets, including the Huffington Post, Vivala, NBC News, and NPR. She has a master of science from Columbia University's Graduate School of Journalism and a bachelor of arts from Rutgers University, where she also taught a journalism course.

Photo Credits

Cover domoyega/E+/Getty Images; p. 5 Donna Ward /Getty Images; p. 9 Srdjan Randjelovic/Shutterstock.com; p. 11 John Lamparski/Getty Images; pp. 14–15 Carolyn A. McKeone /Science Source; pp. 16–17 ink_va/Shutterstock.com; p. 20 Gabe Ginsberg/Getty Images; p. 22 Bertrand Guay/AFP /Getty Images; pp. 26–27, 80 Barcoft Media/Getty Images; p. 33 Africa Studio/Shutterstock.com; pp. 36–37 Westend61 /Getty Images; p. 38 New Africa/Shutterstock.com; p. 41 © iStockphoto.com/Lya_Cattel; p. 44 Likoper/iStock/Thinkstock; pp. 48–49 Stockbyte/Thinkstock; pp. 54–55 RJ Sangosti /The Denver Post/Getty Images; p. 57 Courtesy of Carmen Cusido; pp. 58–59, 75 Monkey Business Images/Shutterstock.com; p. 62 © AP Images; p. 65 Andy Cross/The Denver Post /Getty Images; p. 67 Mark Boster/Los Angeles Times /Getty Images; p. 70 Katarzyna Bialasiewicz/iStock/Thinkstock; p. 73 Phattana Stock/Shutterstock.com; p. 77 Entertainment Pictures/Alamy Stock Photo; pp. 84–85 Mcky Stocker /Shutterstock.com; p. 87 Joe Seer/Shutterstock.com; pp. 88–89 Stephen Brashear/Getty Images.

Design and Layout: Nicole Russo-Duca; Editor: Rachel Aimee; Photo Researcher: Nicole DiMella